SASSY

Saved and Spiritually-Striving Young Women

A guide to help you grow and develop spiritually

Dr. Ruby J. Bowens

Dear Sister Wilma King;
The LORD Jesus
loves you, dearly;
Thank you for your
love + support.
Rev. Ruby J. Bowens

PUBLISHED BY

For more information, contact:
Dr. Ruby J. Bowens
Glorious Gospel Christian Outreach Ministry
227 Iron Street - Loft # 304
Detroit, Michigan 48207

Editorial Development by
Minister Mary D. Edwards, Leaves of Gold Consulting, LLC
LeavesOfGoldConsulting.com

Book cover and page design by
Shannon Crowley for Treasure Image & Publishing
TreasureImagePublishing.com

To my daughter, LaShawn, my sisters, and each of my beautiful nieces as you strive to grow and develop spiritually in your walk with the Lord Jesus.

In memory of my dear mother, Hattie M. Bowens, who introduced me to Jesus,

My dad, Henry Bowens, Jr., who encouraged me to excel academically as a child;

My godmother, Eola Wills for her kindness and prayers, and in memory of our beloved older sister, Brenda, who was SASSY in her own right.

Table of Contents

Introduction

SASSY – **S**aved **a**nd **S**piritually-**S**triving **Y**oung Women was birthed from the mind of God to be written on these pages. The Lord placed on my heart and in my spirit, *SASSY*, in early 2011, and then through the guidance of the Holy Spirit, these acronyms blossomed into *Saved and Spiritually-Striving Young* women. God wishes that no one would perish, but that all would come to repentance (2 Peter 3:9). Sisters, as you are reading these pages, think about the women, young and old, in your circle of life. Although the target group for this writing is to reach young women, spiritually mature women can benefit from and relate to these lessons on how to grow spiritually and to live a saved Christian lifestyle. By sharing with younger women in the body of Christ or a dear sister who wants mentoring, they can learn how to connect with and stay connected to God in their walk with the Lord through the practice of our Christian faith.

INTRODUCTION

SASSY looks at some of the dilemmas young women, who are saved, may find themselves facing and provides some practical ways to connect with their spirituality and strengthen their relationship with the Lord Jesus. The seven topics that will be explored and discussed are 1) Saved and Single; 2) Making Devotional Time a Priority; 3) Handling Peer Relationships; 4) The Courtship; 5) Married Life; 6) God's Destiny for your Life; and 7) Free Indeed.

Each chapter includes biblical foundations. At the end of each chapter, there are sections on Devotional Meditations, Simple Prayers, and Experiential Exercises. There is space for journaling and practical application – *What God wants me to do.* After reading and applying the practical applications of each of the lessons learned, you, or the young woman being mentored, will be on your way to becoming a *SASSY* woman for the Lord! Amen!

CHAPTER ONE

Single & SASSY

There is no shortcut to spiritual formation. This requires a life-long commitment to the disciplines that Jesus, the apostles, and godly followers of the Way, have practiced through the centuries. (Boa 2001, 79)

Reflecting upon that warm, summer day in the afternoon that I accepted Jesus Christ as my Lord and Savior, seems like it was yesterday. I was 12 years old in 1969 and all of us children in the neighborhood were excited about the gifts that would be given out to those who could answer the questions after the bible study lesson. I yearned to learn more about Jesus. I was growing spiritually in love with the Lord.

My mother, Ms. Hattie, as our neighbors and friends would call her, introduced my siblings and me to the Lord as children. We could hear her singing songs of praises to the Lord while cooking dinner in the kitchen. Later, she could be found on her knees praying to the

Lord every night. Mom taught us to pray on our knees at night. She was on her knees praying with us.

At the church on that summer afternoon, I remember sitting there in the class and looking at some of the gifts the evangelist had with him. What caught my eye was a picture of Jesus and His disciples at a table. I did not realize it then, but it was a picture of the Last Supper. The frame around the picture was white and the picture of Jesus and His disciples was painted in bright colors. I really wanted to have this picture. It seemed like eternity had passed before the teacher called on me. I was anxiously raising my hand to answer almost every question. I was afraid the children who answered before me would select the gift that I wanted. Finally, the teacher pointed to me and asked me a question about the lesson.

I answered correctly and he said it was my turn to select a gift. Oh my God! I could *hear* my heart pounding as I walked over and selected the picture of the Last Supper. At the end of the class, the evangelist opened the doors of the church and asked if anyone wanted to be saved. I did! I *accepted* Jesus Christ as my Lord and Savior that day at the young age of 12. This was the beginning of my Christian walk with the Lord. My mother had laid the foundation and I readily confessed Christ to be my Lord. Later, I was baptized.

Living a saved and spiritually-striving lifestyle is a daily walk with the Lord. We are saved and single, now what? The Lord made us unique with our own wonderful personality and has gifted us with spiritual gift(s). We each have our likes and dislikes. We are brilliant, beautiful, bold, and valued in God's eyes; He created us. There may be many questions we may sometimes have about our singleness and salvation. Who am I in God's eyes? One can seek the Lord in prayer and ask Him what His purpose is for your life is; what is your destiny? We are created in God's image and after His likeness to give Him praise. Then God said, "Let us make man in our image, in our likeness . . ." (Gen. 1: 26, NIV). The Holy Spirit is at work in your life transforming it into a Christ-likeness; more into His character.

To strive spiritually, is to seek to connect with God through prayer and meditation on a regular basis. Talking and listening to God is like having a conversation with our parents, who care deeply for us. God is always near and He is ready and waiting to hear from us. He cares for you and me. Prayer is a channel of grace that God has provided for us to connect with Him anytime. We can talk to the Lord about anything that you have a concern about. One question one may ask is, "How do I live as a saved and single, Christian woman?" We can find many answers to our questions in the Bible.

Let's look at what the Lord says to us about who we are as single women and living a holy lifestyle before the Lord. First and foremost, God wants us to love Him with all of our heart and soul, (Matthew 22:37). When we walk with the Lord, we are developing a right relationship with Him. We will come to know His voice and willingly obey Him. The Lord says that the Father is our *husbandman* according to John 15:1. This is to say the Jesus Christ is the True Vine and the Father is Gardner who cares for the branches, that's us, and that makes us fruitful.

When we are growing and productive, this is an indication that we are living a life pleasing to the Lord and are fruitful. The Apostle Paul writes in his epistle to the Romans in Chapter 12:1, 2, you are to "offer your body as living sacrifices, holy and pleasing to God – this is your spiritual act of worship. Do not conform any longer to the pattern of this world, but be transformed by the renewing of your mind." We offer our minds and bodies to God as a sacrifice. This is when the Holy Spirit can do His work in our lives, transforming it into Christ-likeness. When you offer up yourselves as living sacrifices, this mean that you are denying what the flesh wants to do and strive to do those things that are pleasing to God. Know that you cannot do this on our own. You will need the help of the Holy Spirit.

The best China dishes are saved for special occasions, right? One special occasion in life is marriage, which will be discussed later in Chapter Five. First Peter 2:9 says, "But you are a chosen people, a royal priesthood, a holy nation, a people belonging to God, that you may declare the praises of him who called you out of darkness into his wonderful light." Single and saved young women must desire to live a holy lifestyle. As single women who are spiritually striving to please God, let's look to our sisters of antiquity to see how they faced their challenges in life and maintained their spiritual focus. This is good spiritual food on our *fine China!*

Let's look at Rachel. Rachel and Leah, Laban's daughters, were cousins to Esau and Jacob, Isaac and Rebekah's sons. Laban's sister Rebekah was married to Isaac. Rachel, who is described as "lovely in form, and beautiful" (Genesis 29:17), was the desired one for Jacob. (In biblical times, it was their custom to marry other relatives). Rachel is single and the younger of the two sisters. She is a "shepherdess" (Genesis 29: 9). Jacob fell in love with Rachel and was willing to work and wait for seven years for her. As saved and single women who desires to be married, we must *wait* on God's timing to send our husband. Jacob exuded love for Rachel through his patience to wait for her.

As spiritually-striving sisters, patience, which is a part of the Fruit of the Spirit, has to be practiced on a daily basis. While Rachel waited for her betrothed, she was busy working. We, too, must be busy, doing the will of the Lord in our singleness. Our season of singleness is a time of spiritual growth and development. We must learn how to love ourselves for who God had made *us* to be. You are loved by God and are a unique person. From an early age, I knew that I loved Jesus, but I had some spiritual growing to do. I needed to know how to love, emotionally care for and respect myself, and how to please the Lord. Loving oneself is making sure that you are taking care of the body temple. Your spiritual, physical, and mental health is essential to your overall sense of well-being. One can connect with their local community church organization and become active in its ministries. Attend Bible Study classes for spiritual enrichment contributes to our spiritual growth and development. Eating healthier foods and exercise contribute to an overall health and well-being. Exercise can be simply walking for 30 minutes to one hour per day. It strengthens cardiovascular, muscle tone, and respiratory.

Good mental health is most advantageous when we are addressing and handling our stressors or challenges in life in a positive manner. Learning how to recognize the signs or symptoms of depression or anxiety or insomnia, we can address unhealthy feelings early to stay mentally and physically fit. Working through anger or grief and loss issues with the help of others is essential to our good mental health. Seek out a mental health professional if you have questions or experience depression. (References to mental health professionals can be found in the back of this book). Rachel was busy shepherding the sheep. Work can be a joy when you bring a positive mind set to the workplace and you feel good about what you do. As single women, we can take the extra steps to care for ourselves spiritually, mentally, and physically.

Devotional and Meditation

Set aside time each morning or some time during the day when it is quiet and there are no interruptions or distractions to seek God through prayer. Pray and ask the Lord to help you live a life that is pleasing to Him. You may also read Scripture during your devotional time. Talk to God in your own words and tell Him what is on your heart. Be ready to listen for His voice and receive His answer to your prayer request. Now, you must be willing to obey God.

Simple Prayer:

Heavenly Father, I come to you in prayer and ask you, Lord, to show me how to live a holy lifestyle. Lord, your Word says in Romans 12:1, 2, I am to present my body as a living sacrifice, holy and pleasing to you. Lord, I want to please you. Help me Lord. In Jesus Name I ask and pray. Thank God. Amen.

Experiential Exercise:

In order to renew your mind you have to meditate on God's word both day and night. Here are a few Scripture references for you to meditate on for the next thirty days. Genesis 1: 26, 27; Romans 12: 1, 2; Psalm 31: 24; and Psalm 139:14.

SASSY

Notes

Practical Application: *What God wants me to do.*

Chapter Two

Devotional Time & SASSY

A spiritual life is a gift. Henri Nouwen

Oftentimes, I'd wake up early in the morning at the break of dawn. I have grown to pray and thank the Lord for waking me up and keeping me safe throughout night. I would ask God for His guidance and thank Him for my family. Seeking God early where He may be found has been my practice. It is quiet in the early morning hours and I can focus on seeking God's guidance and will for the day. My goal is to spend as much time in prayer and meditation as I can without having a set amount of time to pray; I just pray what is on my heart and invite God's Holy Spirit to come into my presence. I thank the Lord for the brand new day that He has made and has allowed me to live and move and have my being in Him this day. I remember to ask God for forgiveness for sins of omission and for sins of commission - for the things that I did not do and should have done and for the things that I did and was not suppose to do.

Spending time with the Lord each day takes practice and self-discipline. We have to learn how to put our flesh under control. It is easy to become so busy with other things such as work, appointments and schedules, time to workout at the gym, Tuesday night Prayer and Bible study, and spending time with family and friends. Because of our love and reverence for the Lord, we want to draw closer to Him each day through the spiritual disciplines of prayer and meditation. Prayer is a dialogue, not a monologue. It is a two-way communication between God and us. When we pray to the Lord, we then listen for Him to answer our prayers. Sometimes God will initiate the conversation. He oftentimes will speak in a still, small voice. God is Spirit and he speaks to us through our spirits, through His Word, visions or dreams, and through people.

Setting aside devotional time should be a priority every day. Our devotional time may be early in the morning when it is quiet and before our day gets busy. This is a time of acknowledging God and seeking His will for our life during this day and asking in prayer what it is He wants us to do. You can pray and ask God for guidance. He knows the plans that He has for your life. Jeremiah 29:11 tells us what God is saying to us about our life. We can trust God, who created us.

Martha, Mary, and their brother, Lazarus, were friends of Jesus. Jesus was visiting at Martha's home in Bethany. Martha was busying herself with household chores and preparations for her guest. Her younger sister, Mary, sat and listened to what Jesus had to say. Sometimes we can be *so busy cleaning the house* that we miss opportunities to talk to Jesus and to *thank Him for providing the house for us.* Setting priorities and setting aside time to spend with Jesus, your first love, is your priority. Spending time in devotion with Jesus will bring peace to your mind. Jesus gently reminds Martha of what is important. In order to live a saved lifestyle fruitfully, setting aside time to learn what God has planned for us is essential. Being busy can sometimes be a distraction because God is always in communication with us and if we are so busy, the opportunity to hear from God may be missed.

Devote time to talk to God, through prayer, about everything that is on your mind. He knows everything about you; He is your Creator. The Lord God is your First Love. He loves you so much that He sent His only begotten Son, Jesus, to die on the cross at Calvary for the remission of our sins. We read about the life, miracles, death, burial, and resurrection of Jesus Christ in the gospels of Matthew, Mark, Luke, and John. Each of the gospel writers will provide a synoptic or "snapshot" of Jesus' life and ministry.

Gospel writer, John, gives us an "eyewitness" account of Jesus life and crucifixion. John, the beloved disciple, was standing there with Jesus' mother, Mary, and others. Imagine for a moment looking at Jesus dying on the Cross for you. Imagine yourself there. Can you see the blood streaming down from His brow and His body? You have spent time with Jesus and have become friends. Now you have witnessed this awful crucifixion of your friend, Lord and Savior. Christ endured the suffering and died a humiliating death on the cross for you and for me.

Reading books on prayer and meditation can serve as a foundation to help you take the steps to engage in devotion with the Lord on a daily basis. This is spiritual food. Eat everyday to sustain your spiritual well being. As a *SASSY* woman, you will need the Word of God fed (taught) to you on a daily basis to grow up spiritually healthy and fit. Mary chose the better part, according to Jesus, when she took the time to sit at His feet and learn of Him (Luke 10:41).

I have attended many conferences on spiritual growth and development. I have also purchased books on meditation and the other spiritual disciplines, such as prayer, fasting, and worship. We must have a teachable spirit in order to be taught. This takes discipline to take the time to sit and listen and ask questions for a better understanding of the Bible. I remember attending Wednesday night prayer and Bible study at my former church home, East Lake Baptist Church. The pastor taught so powerfully this particular night. As I drove home, all I could think about was what the pastor so aptly taught us. I came into the house and stood at the

TV console and was looking at the photos I had placed there when the Holy Spirit spoke to me and my response was, *"You want me to get my doctorate degree?* The Lord had impressed upon my heart and spirit to go and study at Ashland Theological Seminary. I trusted and obeyed the Lord.

Walking daily with the Lord is a process that begins with our heart's desire to establish a right relationship with the Lord. Jesus stands at the door and knocks (Revelation 3:20).

Take the steps to prioritize and place Jesus at the top of your "to do" list because He is worthy. He sacrificed His own life for the remission of our sins. God sent Jesus, His only begotten Son, because He loves us so dearly. His main focus is you and me. As Jesus hung on the cross at Calvary, His love for us was His priority. He came to save us from this fallen and sin-stained world. Make the decision to spend time with your First Love, Jesus Christ, a priority in your life. He desires a right relationship with us. We are so precious in His sight. When you pray, you can ask God to help you prioritize your daily devotion to Him.

Devotional and Meditation

Set aside time each morning or some time during the day when it is quiet and there are no interruptions or distractions to seek God through prayer. Pray and ask the Lord to help you to set priorities in your life. God understands that there are errands to run, appointments to keep, and work to be completed. Seeking His guidance and allowing Him to direct and guide you will provide you with the inner peace that help keep you focused on what is really important.

Simple prayer:

Heavenly Father, I come to you in prayer asking you to help me to prioritize my day. Lord, I acknowledge you as Father and Lord and you know what really need to get done today. I thank you for your guidance and direction in prioritizing my time, and I trust the outcome of this day to you. It is in Jesus name that I ask and pray. I Thank God. Amen.

Experiential Exercise:

After you pray and ask God to help you prioritize your day, go about completing those things that God has laid on your heart. Mark a place on your calendar at the end of each day. See how the Lord's instructions helped you to prioritize those things that needed to be done and those things that could wait. At the end of thirty days, reflect back and see how the Lord helped you accomplish those things that were important.

Reflect upon how this has strengthened your trust in the Lord to lead and guide you. Practice praying to the Lord and asking Him for guidance every day. Remember that Jesus cares for you. Spending time with the Lord, your First Love, is priority. Here are a few Scripture references for you to meditate on for the next thirty days. Proverbs 3: 5, 6; Psalm 25: 9; Psalm 30: 2; and James 1: 22-25.

SASSY

Notes

Practical Application: *What God wants me to do.*

Chapter Three

Peer Relationships & SASSY

In the process of gaining our rightful place, we must not be guilty of wrongful deeds. Let us not seek to satisfy our thirst for freedom by drinking from the cup of bitterness and hatred. We must forever conduct our struggle on the high plane of dignity and discipline. We must not allow our creative protest to degenerate into physical violence. Again and again, we must rise to the majestic heights of meeting physical force with soul (spiritual) force. (King 1963)

During our lunch hour at Northwestern High School we would walk across the street to the Burger King on Grand River to buy lunch and hang out there with the other students. It would be so nice and sunny outside, we almost did not want to go back into the school building. Have you ever had your best girlfriend call you up and say, "Come on, let's hang out at the mall, or go to a movie, or let's go do ________?" You fill in the blank.

Peer influence is powerful. Can you recall what your momma told you *not to do* and you went ahead and did what you and your girl friends wanted to do when your girl said, "Ahh, come on, we will get back home in time; no one will miss us." Sound familiar? You got back and momma had been looking for you and you perhaps did not tell the whole truth about your whereabouts. Come on, 'fess up!

Many of our younger sisters join gangs to be a part of a family with negative influence. The chain is difficult to break because of the emotional attachment. Some of our young sisters in high school are engaging in lesbian relationships and think that they can go either way and think that it's okay. According to Romans 12: 1, we are to "present your bodies a living sacrifice, holy, acceptable to God." Some of our young sisters may be caught up in the drugs, alcohol, and prostitution. Why is all of this happening? Peer pressure. The sister may have low self-esteem. Teenage pregnancy is on the rise because of poor choices and lack of planning for parenthood.

I remember that beautiful and hot, summer day in 1972, when I was sitting outside on our front porch, minding my own business, and just taking in what a beautiful day it was. I was thanking God for the peacefulness of the day. It was such a peaceful day, and then the devil showed up. He was subtle and unassuming. One of our neighbors, a boy named Jim (all of the names have been changed until God judges the guilty) stopped by and said to me, "come on, take a ride with me over to my sister's house, Ruby, I need to see if she is home." We wrestle not with flesh and blood, but against spiritual wickedness in high places (Ephesians 6:12). The enemy of our souls, the devil, is always busy trying to frustrate the plan of God – the devil comes to steal, kill, and to destroy (John 10:10). God's love for us is more powerful.

I knew Jim. He was quiet and friendly; he laughed and joked with the children on the block. I had no reason to suspect that something was amiss. I did not know that his friend, another boy in the neighborhood named Ryan, who lived down the street from us, had a plan for me. He had approached me weeks before and I had declined his sexual advances. I had forgot about it and focused on my friends. I was not into having casual sex. You know the devil will leave for a season, but he comes back, in a subtle way. I was set up. Here comes Jim on that beautiful summer day asking me to come along as he wanted to *check on his sister.* I went with him; I had let my guard down enjoying the beautiful summer day.

In 1972, at the young age of 16, I was gang raped. I was shaken to my core. It was Ryan, the neighbor down the street, with two other men, waiting for me. Jim had betrayed and set me up. I tried to run out of the house, but they grabbed me before I could get to the door. *God, no, don't let this happen to me, I thought.* I tried to fight them off. My screams for help, my struggling, and cries, went unheard and unnoticed. *No one could hear me.*

My protected world was turned upside down and my eyes were opened to the evil in the world. Through my feelings of shame and guilt, I was unable to tell anyone, what happened to me. *How could I tell mom and hurt her*? I thought.

Peer pressure. Peers have the ability to influence us in a positive or negative way. In my heart, I knew God would take care of them who hurt me. Jim gave me back my clothes and took me back to my house and dropped me off; I felt so much guilt and shame that it was overwhelming. I was *smart*, remember. I had let my guard down – it was *my* fault. I kept going over and over in my mind how could I have been tricked or deceived so easily. I got to the door and opened it and turned and spoke in the universe from the depths of my soul, "God will take care of you all for raping me." Where did this steadfast faith come from at my lowest point? Even in our deepest pain, God is there to comfort us through His Holy Spirit. Although I did not realize it then, my faith in God was real. What my mother taught me about the Lord and His unfailing love for me, as a child, came to my mind. I hid my emotional pain, hurt and disappointment, and wore a mask. I presented a false self to others. I would remember my dad's words when he would always tell me that I was "smart" since I was about four years old.

Jesus brought this word back to my remembrance, when I used to sit in class at Northwestern High School. After the rape, I would go to class and just stare out of the classroom window. I was a good student, why couldn't I focus on my work and complete my assignments, I'd often think to myself. The emotional pain, shame, and guilt that I held inside were eventually too much for me to handle. I left high school eventually. I had pretended to be sick on some days as I would give my mother an excuse not to go to school - me, *the smart one.*

SASSY woman, God is with us in our pain and brokenness; He has experienced the rejection of His own people, pain, and brokenness on His way to the cross to be crucified at Calvary. The Lord Jesus can relate to our pain and suffering. He is our Wounded Healer.

I am again reminded of the words from Dr. Martin Luther King, Jr., written at the beginning of this Chapter, "Again and again, we must rise to the majestic heights of meeting physical force with soul (spiritual) force (King 1963).

Forgiveness means to pardon or excuse a wrong (Matthew 6:12-15). It means to cancel a debt; give up claim for revenge or resentment. To forgive is to trust God and others as if the wrong is forgotten. Re-establish broken relationships. Jesus is speaking in Matthew 6: 14 - 15, and He says, "For if you forgive men when they sin against you, your heavenly Father will also forgive you.

But if you do not forgive men their sins, your Father will not forgive your sins.

God helps us to forgive others. We must be willing participants in the process. We can seek God through prayer and ask Him to help us. This was a thirty year process for me.

Subsequently, I went looking for love in all of the wrong places for comfort from my pain and brokenness. A few years later, I met my daughter's father, who was so kind in the beginning of our relationship. But, the same year, in 1974, that I should have walked across the stage to receive my high school diploma; I gave birth to our daughter, LaShawn. I needed the Lord more than ever now that I was a young mother *and* single. I was not making *smart* choices. I felt lost, lonely, and rejected at times. I was in a lot of emotional pain. To add to my emotional pain, my daughter's father made a lot of promises that he did not keep. I was let down emotionally and mentally when I depended on him; I felt abandoned by him to raise our daughter on my own as a single parent. I sought out the help of a professional therapist.

Help me, Lord, I would pray. I just needed someone to affirm and love me. What did I know about parenting a child? I was barely 18 years old. I thank God for my dear mother, who helped us.

We all have a basic need to be loved and to belong. We must first come into the knowledge that God loves us dearly and He is our First Love (Matthew 6:33). God will never leave us nor forsake us. Be ready and open to having the Holy Spirit direct your life when you are feeling alone, hurt, and rejected. Each of us has a God-given destiny. Your friends' destinies are different from yours. Oftentimes, the Lord purges us from people (our peers) and moves us towards our destiny as we become spiritually mature and yielded to His guidance. You may find yourself saying, *Girl, I don't have time for that anymore.* As a saved and single woman, you should desire to live a life that is pleasing to the Lord. As you grow closer to the Lord, you will find that some places you won't go to anymore and some people you will decide to distance yourself from if they are not following Jesus, who is the Light. If they are not following Jesus, then they are living according to the world's system and bright lights, which are temporal. Jesus' Light is eternal.

The Therapist helped me to find me. I thank God for her as He guided the process. My older brother Drake came over and invited me to church. There, I reconnected to my Lord and Savior Jesus Christ. By the grace of God, I cried out and looked up to the Lord and asked Him to forgive me and to restore me and increase my faith in Him. He did. As saved and single Christian woman, we are married to the Lord. How are we *married* to the Lord? It is a spiritual relationship. In the Gospel according to John 15:1, he writes, "I am the True Vine, and my Father is the husbandman.

Every branch in me that beareth not fruit he taketh away and every branch that beareth fruit, he purgeth it, that it may bring forth fruit" (John 15: 1, 2). Jesus uses this imagery to show His relationship to us. He is the True Vine and we are the branches. God is the Gardener, who cares for and prunes the branches. We are spiritually connected to the Lord. The Holy Spirit is at work in us to transform our life into more Christ-likeness. As we grow and become more spiritually mature, we will be able to demonstrate much of the character of God, which is the work of the Holy Spirit *in us.* The Fruit of the Spirit is love, joy, peace, patience, kindness, goodness, faithfulness, gentleness, and self-control. Against such things there is no law (Galatians 5:22). It is important to surround ourselves with spiritually mature people. Our lifestyles should be pleasing to the Lord. We are in this world, but not of this world. Because we live in a fallen world, there will be trouble. Jesus tells us not to be afraid, He has overcome the world (John 16:33).

Although our peers can influence our behavior if we allow them to, there is nothing that we go through in this life that Jesus did not nail to the Cross at Calvary. "But He was wounded for our transgressions, he was bruised for our iniquity; the chastisement of our peace was upon him; and with his stripes we are healed" (Isaiah 53:5, KJV). The Lord is familiar with grief. I began to yield to the guidance of the Holy Spirit. I prayed to God to help me get my life back. As my spiritual walk with the Lord grew and it became clearer to me that God knew what was best for me, God led me back to school and I completed my high school education in 1978. My self-esteem was high and I was so overjoyed with my accomplishment. The Lord spoke and told me, "Don't stop there." *I decided that I wanted to go to Business College.* I wanted to manage my own business. Remember, we must be *yielded to the guidance* of the Holy Spirit.

I was still a little wobbly in my brokenness, but I knew I was smart; I can do this, I kept telling myself. God kept nudging me to go into "social work." My mind was made up. I was not being disobedient to the Lord; I was focused on protecting myself emotionally. God knew that I was hiding and still wearing a mask because I could not bear to *hear* about anyone else's pain or them being raped, because I was still broken emotionally. So, off to Detroit College of Business I went.

By God's prevenient grace, which is God's grace so freely bestowed upon us, that I earned a Business diploma after one year and an Associate's degree in two years. I was preparing to embark upon earning my BBA, Bachelor of Business Administration, when the Lord started nudging me again to *go into social work.* I willingly yielded to God's nudging, and left Detroit College of Business to enroll in the Bachelor of Social Work Program at University of Detroit Mercy. I thought, *I wonder what I will learn from this school* as I walked up those stairs to enroll. Four years later in May 1996, I was graduated from U of D Mercy, *Magnum Cum Laude* with my Bachelor's of Social Work degree. This was such a positive and challenging experience for me. I worked during the day for the Detroit Board of Education as a Secretary and I attended the University of Detroit Mercy at night. I was determined to succeed. I remembered that I "was smart" from my dad's early encouragement and the Lord saying, "Don't stop there" after I completed my high school education. *Girl, I don't have time for that anymore* was the story of my life. I was attuned to the Spirit who was guiding my life. I was a *SASSY* woman. I literally did not have time to spare. I had my daughter to raise and thank God for mom and my family for helping us. I was employed full-time with the Detroit Board of Education as a secretary, and I was carrying a full load of classes, 12 credits, at night.

God has a plan for me and God has a plan for your life, too. God led me to enroll immediately in the Master of Social Work Program at Wayne State University. I was prepared, in my senior year at U of D Mercy, to go right into the Advanced Standing Master's of Social Work Program at Wayne State University in June 1996. I was graduated from Wayne State University in May 1997 with my Master of Social Work degree. When God moves, we are to move with Him with a sense of urgency and purpose. You must learn how to tune into God; have a discerning ear to hear His voice. God can speak through the noise and other voices we hear in our head, e.g., got to pick up my child at 6:00 p.m., mother needs her prescription; remember to mail the check for the utilities, and so on. Can we hear God through the noise?

As was mentioned in Chapter Two, devotional time with the Lord is essential to our faith walk. I had developed the time to devote to the Lord and meditate. It was five years later, I remember that the Holy Spirit laid on my heart to go and get my doctorate degree at Ashland Theological Seminary. I was excited and was graduated with my doctor of ministry degree in May 2007. God has a plan and a purpose for our lives (Jeremiah 29, 11).

Over thirty years had passed since the rape occurred. I recalled that one of my classroom assignments at Seminary was to lead a small group. The professor has assigned the topics to each student and my topic was, *"Emotions, can you trust them?"* Lord, am I going to have to talk about the rape? I thought. As I began to prepare for the group, God was speaking and assuring me that "yes," I was going to talk about the rape. Little did I know that God was preparing me for my healing and deliverance from over 30 years of emotional pain and brokenness after being raped when I was 16 years old. I wore a mask; I was in bondage. But, I still belonged to God!

The devil thought he had me, *but God!* Yes, I was *smart* and excelled academically, only because of the Lord's amazing grace. I had a daughter to take care of and children have a way of helping you to grow up when you are responsible for their care. God had a purpose and plan for my life.

That small group in Seminary was God opening the door and setting me free. *I am free*! I cried, no longer bound – no more chains holding me – Praise the Lord, Hallelujah, I'm free! The mask came off that day and I was free to be me and tell others how God had healed me. I could talk about the rape and tell others what happened to me when I was sixteen years old and what it cost me. I had forgiven those who caused all of this pain in my life. The Scripture teaches that "For we wrestle not with flesh and blood, but against the rulers, against the authorities, against the powers of this dark world and against the spiritual forces of evil in the heavenly realms" (Ephesians 6: 12). The group members all surrounded me with love and the Holy Spirit moved in that room and deliverance took place. The tears ran down my face and it felt like a very heavy burden was lifted from my shoulders. I received my healing in that small group in Seminary. A burden I had held inside for over 30 years. I have to give all glory to God. He carried me!

When I returned home from Seminary, I called my now adult daughter, LaShawn, and told her what happened to me when I was 16 years old. I thank God for healing me and setting me free. I told my mother and she showed love and concern for me. Of course she looked at me and asked why I did not tell her. God knows. God works things out for our good. I told others in my family, my friends, and they were happy for me and comforted and supported me. I was attuned to Jesus and what He wanted for *my* life. We have to tell friends and peers sometimes that, *Girl, I don't have time for that anymore* when we follow Jesus.

There will be a separation from some people, from what we used to do, and from where we used to go. God's plan for our lives is perfect. God knows the plans that He has for our lives (Jeremiah 29:11). God remembers. I no longer wear a mask. I am *SASSY* for Jesus! The devil no longer has a stronghold over me. One of the lyrics in the song "I almost let go" says, *"The devil thought he had me, but God came and grabbed me and held me close."* God broke the devil's grip and set me free.

Devotional and Meditation

During your devotional and meditation, seek God and ask Him if there is anything in your life that needs to be healed. Ask Him is there people in your life that do not contribute to your spiritual growth and development, but they deplete you; only take what they can get. You may know of the area in your life where you have been wounded and broken by peers, in a bad relationship, or through a hurtful experience. Ask God to heal your wounded, broken spirit and set you free from the bondage and stronghold of the devil. Ask God if there is any unforgiveness in your life. Ask God to first forgive you and to help you to forgive those who hurt you.

Simple prayer:

Heavenly Father, I come to you in prayer asking you to reveal to me any area in my life now, my childhood, and past relationships with my friends and peers, where I was hurt or deeply disappointed where I need Your healing touch. Lord, I need a touch from You.

There is healing in Your blood, Jesus. I want to be free, Lord, open my eyes to see. Liberate me God from the snares of the devil. I need to be free to worship You, Lord, in spirit and in truth. I want healing in my mind, healing in my body temple, healing in my relationships. Lord, please forgive me of my sins, and I release and forgive those who hurt or disappointed me. I want to grow spiritually, Lord. In Jesus Name I pray and Thank God. Amen.

Experiential Exercise:

After you pray and ask God for forgiveness, ask Him to reveal the brokenness in your life, meditate on the following Scriptures as you are waiting to hear from the Lord. Read these Scriptures for the next thirty days to get them in your spirit. Be ready to be set free. The Scripture references are: Proverbs 3: 5, 6; Psalm 139; Matthew 5:44; and Romans 12:1.

SASSY

Notes

Practical Application: *What God wants me to do.*

Chapter Four

Courting & SASSY

. . . God always meets us where we are and slowly moves us along into deeper things. Occasional joggers do not suddenly enter an Olympic marathon. They prepare and train themselves over a period of time, and so should we... This comes as a genuine liberation to many of us, but it also set tremendous responsibility before us. We are working with God to determine the future! (Foster 1998, 35)

Waiting on the Lord and praying to Him for a saved husband can seem like eternity. God's timing is different from ours. God works through *kairos.* We have a tendency to look at our biological clocks and the clocks on the wall. God is never late; He is always on time. Kairos means simply that God *steps in time.* He transcends and is not bound by our chronological time. Waiting on the Lord does not mean being idle until God shows up with the blessing. God honors our faith. Faith, without works is dead, according to James 2:17.

Faith requires belief that God can bring *it* to pass. Hebrews 11:1 says, "Faith is the substance of things hoped for and the evidence of things not seen. While you are waiting on God to manifest His promises to you, get busy serving God and others.

Ruth, a Moabite woman, became widowed when her husband died. She clung to her mother-in-law, Naomi, because she had bonded with her and had a desire to know about her mother-in-laws' God. Ruth loved her mother-in-law, Naomi. Recently widowed, Ruth begged to stay with Naomi wherever she went, even though it would mean leaving her homeland. In heartfelt words Ruth said, "Your people will be my people and your God my God" (Ruth 1:16). Naomi agreed, and Ruth traveled with her to Bethlehem. A lot is said about Naomi who loved and cared for Ruth. Obviously, Naomi's life was a powerful witness to the reality of God.

Ruth was drawn to her mother-in-law and to the God she worshipped. In the succeeding months and years, God led this young Moabite widow to a man named Boaz, whom she eventually married. As a result, she became the great-grandmother of David and an ancestor in the line of the Messiah. What a profound impact Naomi's life made!

What does your Christian witness look like; Now that you are *SASSY*, a Saved, and Spiritually-Striving Young Woman? Get busy telling others about Jesus. Tell others what the Lord has done for you. You are now on your way to investing your time in devotion and study (2 Tim. 2:15).

Before Ruth knew it, her mother-in-law had sent her to glean in her relative's field. Ruth was busy gleaning for wheat and barley that fell to the ground. She did not know who Boaz was and that he had inquired of her through his foreman. While you are busy doing the Lord's work, God will position you for your husband to find you. He, who finds a wife, finds a good thing and obtains favor from the Lord according to Proverbs 18:22. Notice that the man *finds* a wife. The saved and spiritually-striving young woman is found faithful busy doing the Lord's work before she becomes the *wife.*

God has now sent the man into your life, *finally!* The courtship is the time to get to know one another. You both know that this is a God-connection and marriage is on the horizon, but you want to know more about each other naturally. As a *SASSY* woman, you are maintaining your devotional life to the Lord. You are busy doing the Lord's work, and sharing some of your time with your husband-to-be, at this point in the courtship, getting to know one another. This is a good time to spend with each others' families and getting to know them, too. Observe how he relates to God, his mother, and women relatives in his life. You can learn a whole lot about him.

He can learn more about you, as well. As a *SASSY* woman, God will provide more opportunities for you to grow spiritually as you and your husband-to-be grow closer in your courtship and faith walk with God. The man is the head; God made him the head and created him first. Refer to Genesis 1:27, 28. We are a help mate to our husbands. We are equal in the relationship and marriage, but God has given the man the authority to be the head and priest of his family.

Ruth and Boaz eventually marry and I will discuss more about their relationship and marriage in the next chapter on *Married and SASSY.*

Why do you think it is important that you as *SASSY* women allow the Lord to choose your husband for you? Naturally, there is a tendency to look through our natural eyes. We see the outward appearance, but God sees the heart and He knows the plans that He has for our lives and what is best for each of us. God knows us, our thinking patterns, likes, and dislikes, weaknesses, and strengths. He knows our inner most being (Psalm 139). God has a husband *just for you and for me.* I feel a shout coming on! God has equipped me with the education and spiritual tools needed to help guide others, like you, *SASSY* woman, on the spiritual journey. Look where the Lord has brought me from! Keep busy and wait on God's timing, *kairos.* The busyness is purposeful and productive. As you are connected with your local church ministry, there will be many opportunities for you to get involved. Your husband-to-be may be involved with the choir or youth ministry or a pastor. He may teach or coach a youth basketball team for the church. Use your ministry gifts to lift up the body of Christ and to give God glory.

Remember, your husband and you are *courting*, therefore honor God in your courtship and *wait on the Lord* until your marital vows are legal. Marriage is honorable in God's sight and the bed is undefiled. Amen! Wait on the Lord and be of good courage. Wait for your wedding day!

Devotion and Meditation:

During your daily devotional time, pray and ask God to continue to keep you holy and pure. With God's help, we can do all things through Christ, which strengthens us (Phil. 4:13). Ask God to strengthen your faith, your love for your husband-to-be, and your friendship. As you draw closer to God, ask God to help you and your husband-to-be to stay focused on the work of ministry that the Lord is calling you both too.

Simple Prayer:

Heavenly Father, thank you for my husband you have chosen for me. I pray, Lord, that I will honor and respect my husband, love, support, and encourage him each day. Lord, I pray for our spiritual growth together, for our lives and love for each other, our friendship, relationship, spiritual growth, and prayer life. Help us, dear Lord, to both look to you for guidance and to pray to you before making decisions.

Experiential Exercise:

Pray this prayer each day for thirty days to strengthen your prayer life and walk with God and to keep God before you as you prepare for your wedding day. Scripture References: Mark 11: 22, John 9:1-41. Genesis 2:18; Ephesians 5:24; Proverbs 31: 31, and 1 Peter 3: 1, 2.

SASSY

Notes

Practical Application: *What God wants me to do.*

Chapter Five

Married & SASSY

In season and out of season, generation after generation, faithful women and men turn to the Psalms as a most helpful resource for conversation with God about things that matter most. (Brueggemann, 2001, 1)

It's time to pull out the best China! Marriage is God's idea and truly a special occasion and almost every girl's dream is to be married. I recently attended a Women's Conference sponsored by my church's women's ministry and participated in the workshop entitled, *Marriage.* In the group, were *married* and single women, who talked about their marriage, its challenges and benefits, and those who were still single talked about their desire to be *married. SASSY* women can benefit from the life and experiences of others. The married women in the group were married for 30 years or more. Some of the women were widowed or divorced; others were still in their marriages.

As *SASSY* women desiring to be married, while you are single, Christ is your husbandman as you learned in Chapter One. Christ is the True Vine and the Father is the Gardner who prunes the branches (Christians) to make them fruitful. Those branches that are not fruitful, He cuts off.

You want to be fruitful doing the work of ministry up to your wedding day and beyond.

I've seen what a successful marriage looks like and what a dysfunctional marital relationship looks like. I have learned through the sharing of married women, that the marital relationship *takes work*. It takes work from both sides and communication is one of the main components. We cannot read another person's mind, nor can you expect him to *figure out how we are feeling*. In a relationship context, you have to communicate with each other.

Looking at Queen Esther's role in the Persian Empire under King Xerxes, she risked her own security and life for those of her Jewish brothers and sisters. Her husband was Xerxes, the King of Persia. In the Jewish tradition, if the King had not requested Esther to come into his presence, she was not allowed. Esther is described as courageous and a careful planner. We can read about Queen Esther in the Old Testament Book of Esther.

Romance and intimacy are healthy components of marriage. Christ is at the Center, and it has to be balanced with compatibility, communication, comfort, and commitment, the five C's. Trust is another important component. It is vital to seek God's guidance for Him to choose our husband; God looks upon the heart. We see with our natural eyes. This was discussed in Chapter four.

Queen Vashti refused to obey a command from her husband, King Xerses, King of Persia. Because of her refusal to submit to her husband's demands, she was deported from the palace and the King searched for a new wife. Enter Queen Esther. This is a story of intrigue, power, and drama (Book of Esther).

In today's society, it is not that easy to just send the wife away and look for a new one. Marriage is good and honorable and is God's idea. According to Matthew 19:6, marriage is permanent and is based on the principled practice of love, not on feelings alone. Look at Boaz and Ruth's relationship.

As I reflect upon my parents' marriage when I was a young child, I remember that we used to go to Belle Isle and have family outings often during the summer months. Spending time with your spouse and family strengthens the relationship through comfort and communication. You affirm each other as you set aside time to really find out what is going on in your family's life. My dad, Henry, would pick me up and as we walked across the Belle Isle (MacArthur) Bridge and put me on his shoulders and he would ask me, "Can you swim?" With my five year-old voice, I responded, "Nooooo" looking at all of that water in the Detroit River and clinging to my daddy's neck.

The husband that loves the Lord first and is spiritually mature will know how to treat, honor, and respect, his wife, and family. He honors and loves God and wants to do those things that please the Lord; he has a healthy reverence for the Lord. The spiritually mature husband will cherish and honor his God-sent wife. Trust is an important component in a marriage. Without trust, there will be a breakdown in communication, comfort, commitment, and compatibility. During the courtship stage, trust is developed. It is vital to be trustworthy yourself in your marriage as a saved and spiritually-striving woman of God. Trust takes time to develop in a relationship and going forward into a marriage. It is essential that trust is established. It is difficult to relate to a person whom you do not trust. You will always have up an invisible wall to protect yourself. You will hide things to keep them safe and secure. You will be anxious and worried, and become distracted thinking about the untrustworthy person left in your home alone, or so you think. Trusting God with all of your heart, your soul, and your mind, is necessary to spiritual growth and development (Proverbs 3: 5, 6). When relationships fail, God never fails.

Devotion and Meditation:

During your daily devotional time, pray and ask God for your husband. Pray for his faith walk, his health and strength, his mind and continued spiritual growth with the Lord. Pray that your husband will have eyes only for you. Pray that the Lord would anoint his head and feet to walk in God's precepts. Pray for your husband and the protection of your marriage and what God has joined together, let no one separate. You can trust God and depend upon Him. Pray that you have open communication with one another and there is nothing hidden. Pray to grow to trust your husband. In Jesus' Name. Amen.

Simple Prayer:

Heavenly Father, I honor and acknowledge You as Lord. I thank you in advance for choosing my husband for me. A man after Your own heart; a man who loves and reverences You first, Lord. You know his heart and Lord, You know what I need in a mate and in my marriage. I ask that you choose my husband for me, Lord. You know all about me and I pray and ask You, Lord, for my husband who is a perfect fit for me. Thank you, Heavenly Father. In Jesus' Name I ask and pray. I thank God. Amen.

Experiential Exercise:

Pray and seek out married couples in your family and in the church congregation and ask them if you can talk with them about marriage. Ask questions on how they honor God in their marriage, what the challenges are and what are the rewards and benefits. Take notes for your future reference. SASSY women, you are loved by God.

SASSY
Notes

Practical Application: ***What God wants me to do.***

CHAPTER SIX

God & SASSY

God is all-seeing, all-knowing, all-powerful, and everywhere present. God knows us, God is with us, and his greatest gift is to allow us to know him. (NIV Commentary)

King David wrote in Psalm 139:13-16,

> *"For you created my inmost being; you knit me together in my mother's womb. I praise you because I am fearfully and wonderfully made; your works are wonderful, I know that full well. My frame was not hidden from you when I was made in the secret place. When I was woven together in the depths of the earth, your eyes saw my unformed body. All the days ordained for me were written in your book before one of them came to be" (NIV).*

God know the plans that He has for you, *SASSY* woman, and He knew those plans before the whole world was framed. Oftentimes, you may want to plan the course for your life, but once you realize and acknowledge God as Creator, through knowledge of Him and spiritual maturity, you will submit your will and plans for your life to God, for He knows the plans He has ordained just for you (Jeremiah 29:11).

In my brokenness emotionally, I recall that I still had the dream tucked away in my heart to go to college and obtain a business degree in management. I had a desire to own and manage my own business one day. I remember my dad telling me since I was four years old, that I was *"smart."* You know the enemy, the devil, will try to deceive you and influence your mind. The devil's desire is to "sift you as wheat" (Luke 22:31) and to frustrate the plan of God for your life - but, to no avail. We have the victory through Christ Jesus! I realize that it was God speaking through my dad when my dad was telling me, "You're smart" at a young age. I did not feel *smart* when I was deceived by my neighbor to, "Come on, and take a ride with me over to my sister's house." I had no reason to be suspicious of this brother; we knew each other's families and all of the neighborhood kids, *or so I thought.* But, I *believe* God!

The overwhelming guilt and shame was devastating for me as you read in Chapter Three. God's plan for your life will be accomplished. Do not be deceived by the devil. Just because you made one, two, or three mistakes in your life does not mean that your life is over. You can start over, but you have to realize that you can't do it on your own. You don't have to. The Holy Spirit is in us to help us and to guide us towards God's purposes and plans for our lives. No matter what the situation or the circumstances are, God is a real big God who heals broken hearts and forgives us of all our transgressions. Go to God in prayer and watch how He changes things.

God spoke to me through the pain and guided me back to school. I excelled academically by the grace of God and I believed that I could do it and that I *was smart* enough to accomplish what God had laid on my heart. God has taken my life and has made something beautiful out of it. I can look in the mirror and see myself as a *SASSY* woman and I thank God for saving me and you can too! What God has done for me, God will do the same for you. Only believe!

SASSY woman, if you have been through challenging times and trials, and you are reading the pages in this book or are being mentored by a mature *SASSY* Sister, know that God has a plan for your life. Know that you are predestined for greatness *SASSY* woman; that you can do *all things through Christ who gives you the strength* (Philippians 4:13). *That you are more than a conqueror through Christ Jesus* who loves you (Romans 8:37), and you are *fearfully and wonderfully made by God* (Psalm 139:14). No matter what your former lifestyle may have been or what you have done in the past, God's eyes are on you; He has never left you and He never will. God wants a right relationship with you; talk with Him often through prayer and meditation. I encourage you to walk towards your destiny in God. Keeping on walking with the Lord, *SASSY* woman; no turning back! What the Lord has for you, it is for you. No devil can take it, snatch it, change it, or prevent it. What God has promised you, *SASSY*, God will bring it to pass.

God's word is true, *it will come to pass.* Wait on the Lord, be of good courage, again I say, wait on the Lord. While you are waiting on the Lord to bring His promises to pass in your life, serve God and others. God has blessed you to be a blessing. Seek out volunteer opportunities or serve on the Missions Ministry with your local church. People are hurting all over the world. Just turn on the local news and see and hear the many tragic stories that touch people's lives everyday.

Always seek God's face through prayer to see where He is guiding you (Matthew 6:33). When God gives vision, God gives provision. I have been working on this particular job for almost two years as the Clinical Supervisor when I heard that our program would be re-organized and my position was in jeopardy. I went into prayer to ask God what I should do. I was about to lose my livelihood. Should I start looking for another place of employment and leave this position before I receive my pink slip? Well, God in His infinite wisdom responded to me and told me to move across the hall into the office that was supposed to my office when we first moved to this new location almost a year and a half earlier. The office was already vacant since the program manager who occupied the office had been pink slipped already. I asked permission to move across to the new office from the new administrator and she said "yes" that I could move to the other office.

It was November 2009, four months before I would lose my job that I am working in my new office and I started training my staff to continue to facilitate groups, chair the weekly staff meetings, and instructed them on how to prepare the weekly report for our contractors. It's called succession planning. You have to think about others in the midst of your storm. God will take care of you. I needed to ensure that the program would continue to operate at it optimum after my employment terminated.

You may ask, *SASSY woman,* why would I care? I am losing my job. You have to know who you are in Christ Jesus. When God closes one door, God will open another one. Think about other's well being first and God will not forget about you.

In March 2010, on a Friday afternoon, I was told by the new administrator that my services were no longer needed. I went to my office to box up my belongings. I felt sad, but confident that I had worked there and honored God. I left with a sense that I had done my best. Tuesday morning of the following week, I opened up my e-mail and to my surprise there was an official invitation from Sabrina, my friend, sister, and colleague in the ministry. The invitation was inviting me to travel on a foreign missions trip to Haiti. An informational meeting will be held *that night* at 7:00 p.m. Before I could form the words to the prayer that I was about to ask God, my heart was shouting, *I'm going to Haiti!* Talk about God's destiny for our lives! God is always moving on our behalf.

The information meeting that night was so insightful and exciting. After I left the meeting, while driving home on the freeway in my mini-van, I started praising God for what He was doing in my life. One door was recently shut and now God was opening up a real BIG door for me to travel abroad. My God! I had just lost my livelihood and God was preparing to send me to Haiti to help others. When God gives vision, He gives provision. I did not even think about where the finances would come from; I just trusted God. We were instructed to write letters and ask for sponsorship for the trip. I took the letter to my pastor, Lawrence T. Foster, who fully and prayerfully supported me. He lifted it up to the church congregation and other colleagues in the ministry. They responded with such love and financial support that I was completely awed by God. It's *a God thing* when people can come together and help one another.

Haiti was devastated by a 7.0 earthquake in January 2010. The city of Port-au-Prince was devastated. Lives were lost, houses crumbled, schools and church buildings were impacted by the earthquake. The people of Haiti were shaken to their core. They were looking for loved ones buried under the rubble. In a matter of seconds, their lives were turned upside down. Ten to twelve of us missionaries from the United States traveled to Haiti in June 2010 to bring hope and a sense of restoration through training on trauma and grief and loss.

Our mission was to train the Haitians to identify stagnated grief and loss within their communities and be able to address it through grief counseling. We are committed to follow-up with our brothers and sisters in Haiti over the next few years. God knows the plans He has for your life, *SASSY* woman. You may experience being hurt, disappointed, and rejected. Through all of this, God's plans for your life will prevail. Look to the Lord in every situation that you face. Ask God, "What would you have me to do? Listen for His instructions. God is positioning you, *SASSY*, for success.

Devotion and Meditation:

During your devotional time with the Lord, meditate on listening for God's voice. God speaks through His Word, to our spirits, and may confirm His Word through other people. Meditation is listening for God's voice. Meditate on Philippians 4:19.

Simple Prayer:

Heavenly Father, thank you for the plans that You have for my life. No matter what I may be facing in this world, I know that You know the plans that You have for me; plans to prosper me and not harm me. You have plans to give me a hope and a future. (Jeremiah 29:11). Thank You, Heaven Father, for your plans for my life. Help me to live the life You have created and ordained for me to live. I thank You and praise You. In Jesus name I pray and thank God. Amen.

Experiential Exercise:

Write down the instructions you sense God placing on your heart. This way you can refer to it later. Be mindful to follow God as He is guiding you. Trusting God is a process. Once you believe that you do trust God, then it become easier to follow Him. Take the steps that the Lord instructs you to do. When you pray, this will cancel out worry about how you are going to make it or where are the finances coming from. Meditate on Psalm 23.

SASSY

Notes

Practical Application: ***What God wants me to do.***

Chapter Seven

Free & SASSY

As the hart panteth after the water brooks, so panteth my soul after thee, O God. My soul thirsteth for God, for the living God: when shall I come and appear before God? (Psalm 42, KJV).

SASSY woman, you are walking with the Lord on a daily basis. Now you understand that this is a faith walk and that you trust God in everything. I am reminded of a song that my pastor, Lawrence T. Foster, had given to the minister of music to sing at my dear mother's home-going service in October 2009 called "I am Free." The lyrics says, "*I am free, no longer bond - I'm free, no more chains holding me. My soul is resting, it's just a blessing, praise the Lord, Hallelujah, I'm free.*" The song does wonders to lift one's spirit. When you think about the Lord and His goodness, it makes you want to shout, "GLORY, AND THANK YOU, JESUS."

I thank the Lord for my dad and my mom. I thank Him for my dad for his early encouragement and telling me "Ruby, you are smart." I thank God for my mother who introduced my brothers and sisters and me to Jesus at a young age. I thank God for Jesus, who did not come down from the Cross at Calvary, but saw you, *SASSY* woman, and me, and suffered and died for the remission of sins. And because of the cross work on Calvary, you and I have a right to eternal life. Free and free indeed! Whom the Son has set free is free indeed.

SASSY, don't go back into bondage, but rather walk in the narrow way of the Lord. Be a light for Jesus, who is the Light of this world. He will point you in the way that you should go. As you trust Jesus and obey His commands, your life will be pleasing to Him. We are the salt of the earth and light. You, *SASSY* woman, are an ambassador for the Lord. When you walk into a room, people should notice something different about you before you even speak.

And when you speak *SASSY* woman, it is always out of love and reverence for the Lord Jesus. As the deer thirsts for water, your soul should thirst for God (Psalm 42). Daily you are connecting to the Lord through devotion, prayer, meditation, and sometimes fasting. Fasting is a way to push the plate away and pray to God for insight or for an answer to a particular situation. Consult with your spiritual leader about fasting.

Jesus Christ died for your sins. You are no longer under the power of sin that comes in your life to tempt you. You have a way of escape. Jesus Christ, the One who was victorious on the cross at Calvary and over death, hell, and the grave, will give you the grace to stand on His Word and on His promises. Remind yourself of what the Psalmist wrote in Psalm 61:2, 3, "Lead me to the rock that is higher than I. For you have been my refuge, a strong tower against the foe."

In Chapter Three, you read about how you will lose some friends on your spiritual walk with the Lord. You won't have time for the same old things that you used to do as God moves you towards your destiny. As you grow closer to the Lord, you will find that some places you won't desire to go to anymore and some people you will distance yourself from. Your interests will change as you grow spiritually closer to the Lord. You should desire to live a life that is pleasing to the Lord.

SASSY woman, you are free indeed to live the life the Lord has predestined you to live in Him. It is not a freedom to give place to the flesh, but rather a freedom to choose to be the righteousness of God. Surround yourself with people of like mind who will encourage you in your faith walk. If you are unsure of your election in Christ, *SASSY,* the world will pull you back to the former things. Your desire is to remain steadfast and abound in your faith.

In my Christian experience over the years, I have seen people come into the church and start serving the Lord and then I don't see them for a while. Others would come into the church and start serving and stay committed. People do struggle with their spirituality. There is a war between the spirit and the flesh. The Apostle Paul reminds us that we are not to conform to this world; this place is not our home. You, *SASSY* woman, are to be transformed and to renew your mind (Romans 12: 1, 2). It is not an option. Satan desires to sift you like wheat. In John 10:10, Jesus says that the devil comes to steal, kill, and to destroy. But Jesus has come that we may have life and have it more abundantly.

Devotion and Meditation:

In your daily devotion, meditate on where the Lord has brought you from in your spiritual walk with the Lord. This will keep things in perspective. It has not been easy to get where you are now. There have been many snares and traps, but the Lord kept you safe.

Simple Prayer:

Pray the prayer of Thanksgiving. You are thankful for your relationship with the Lord and for your family and friends. Thank the Lord for spiritual growth and development and from setting you free from the enemy and anything that would distract or keep you from serving God. In Jesus' Name. Amen!

Experiential Exercise:

Write down the many blessings that the Lord has bestowed upon you just this past year. You know that these things were the Lord's doing. You realize that if it had not been for the Lord opening the door and making a way, it would not have been done. As you write, reflect upon the Lord's goodness, grace, and mercy. This will help to keep things into perspective as you realize the Lord's presence in your life.

SASSY

Notes

Practical Application: *What God wants me to do.*

Prayerful Thoughts for You

I hope and pray that you have been inspired as you read these pages. "The formation of a spiritual life begins with changing familiar ways of thinking and behaving and aligning one's will with the will and plan of God" (Bowens 2007, 83).

SASSY woman, please share this spiritual guide with your sisters or girlfriends who are *SASSY*. Mentor a struggling young woman who desires a closer walk with the Lord. I prayed to the Lord, as I wrote these words to you, that the Lord would speak to you and continue to comfort and guide you towards your destiny. I will continue to pray that this little book, with big blessings, would touch the hearts and minds of God's daughters everywhere as we are *SASSY women*! You may continue to practice the experiential exercises as often as you desire. Pray the simple prayers to the Lord often as God desires a right relationship with you. Prayer is a channel of grace that the Lord has provided for you to connect with Him. Meditate on the Word of God and listen as God speaks to you, then obey Him. Do what God tells you to do. Continue to work out your salvation (Philippians 2:12, 13). If you find yourself hurt, bound, and disappointed, be reminded that Jesus has overcome the world. Go to Him in prayer and meditation. Tell God where it hurts. Jesus is a Healing Balm in Gilead. Give it all to Him for He cares for you.

My prayer for you, *SASSY* woman, is to be steadfast, unmovable, always abounding in the work of the Lord. Please know that your work is not in vain in the Lord (1 Corinthians 15:58). Remember to keep Jesus on your journey. You, *SASSY* woman, are victorious in Christ Jesus. Do not look at where you have been or what you have done or what was done to you, but rather look to God, the Author and Finisher of our faith. "There is therefore now no condemnation for those who are in Christ Jesus" (Romans 8:1). I realize that I was not a victim, but I am VICTORIOUS IN CHRIST JESUS. I am alive today because of God's grace and mercy. The devil wanted to frustrate the plan of God, but he could not do it. Jesus defeated him on the cross at Calvary. Jesus paid it all for us, *SASSY* woman. We belong to God! "Yea, though I walk through the valley of the shadow of death, I will fear no evil; for Thou art with me; thy rod and thy staff they comfort me" (Psalm 23:4).

From the Author:

I give honor and glory to God who has made this literary work possible. The birthing process was arduous and emotional, yet rewarding. I would like to thank my family for their prayers and support they have given me. I pray that as you read the words on these pages, that the Lord would touch your life in a supernatural way. I pray also for the salvation of all God's *SASSY* daughters in the Lord as you yield and allow the Holy Spirit to transform your lives. Please contact your local community mental health agency for mental health intervention with depression or grief and loss concerns. I would like to thank God for my editor, Mary Edwards, Leaves of Gold Consulting, and publisher, Shannon Crowley, Treasure Image Publishing, for their love, words of encouragement, and the wonderful work they do.

You may call my prayer line at (313) 258-1511 for prayer and spiritual guidance. For the unsaved sisters, are you ready to accept Jesus Christ as your Lord and Savior? Pray this prayer: **Father, in the Name of Jesus, I ask that You please forgive me of my sins. I repent of my**

sins and confess with my mouth that Jesus is Lord and I believe in my heart that Jesus died for the remission of my sins on the cross at Calvary and that God raised Him from the dead on the third day (Romans 10:9,10). Hallelujah, you are saved this day! I am praying for you.

Bibliography

Bible, The Holy. 2003. King James Version. Thomas Nelson Bibles. A Division of Thomas Nelson, Inc.

Bible, Life Application Study. 1991. New International Version. Wheaton, IL: Tyndale House Publishers, Inc.

Bible, The Wesley Study Bible. 1989. New Revised Standard Version. Nashville, TN: Abingdon Press.

Boa, Kenneth. 2001. *Conformed to His image*: Biblical and practical approaches to spiritual formation. Grand Rapids, MI: Zondervan Publishing House.

Bowens, Ruby J. 2007. *The impact of the practice of spiritual disciplines on the self-image of adult male substance abusers in treatment.* Dissertation - Ashland Theological Seminary, Ashland, OH.

Brueggeman, Walter. 2001. *The spirituality of the Psalms.* Minneapolis, MN: Fortress Press.

Foster, Richard. 1983. *Celebration of discipline: The path to spiritual growth.* New York, NY: HarperCollins.

King Jr., Martin Luther. 1963. *I have a dream.* americanrhetoric.com.

Nouwen, Henri J. M., 1981. *Making all things new.* New York, NY: HarperCollins Publishers, Inc.

To order additional copies
Contact Dr. Ruby J. Bowens
(313) 258-1511
bowensruby@aol.com

Made in the USA
Charleston, SC
15 July 2016